S. E. Haist

Painting in the Chinese Manner

SHU-CHI CHANG

Painting in the Chinese Manner

ENGLISH TEXT BY HELEN F. CHANG

A STUDIO BOOK

THE VIKING PRESS · NEW YORK

First published in 1960 by The Viking Press, Inc.
625 Madison Avenue, New York 22, N.Y.

Published simultaneously in Canada by
The Macmillan Company of Canada Limited

Library of Congress catalog card number: 60–14089

Printed in the U.S.A. by The Murray Printing Company

PREFACE

How can I answer the questions so often asked during my twelve years of life in America? Is there a way to show my friends how I paint, combining with modern techniques the traditional methods of my ancestors?

Chinese paintings and painting procedures are often described in lofty and mystifying terms, which may fail to tell the student what he most wishes to learn. In the pages that follow I shall endeavor to discuss in detail the procedures I have followed, and shall use some of my paintings as examples. If I can write a statement at once simple and informative, perhaps it will tell the artist and the art lover alike how to paint in the Chinese manner.

CONTENTS

書旅書畫法

張書旅

吾國畫學浩如淵海綜其物筆皆首推工次非尖尖簡單坐求可畫至邊

作走以發揚之

染二章至于氣韻生動屬繪畫之目的而非法則故不列入得求此者

乙章即獨營位置是四隨摹一章即傳模移寫是也此外另加用其道

化三章即說明應物象形之理由色彩用墨三章即隨類傳彩之意也三章法

目的者四此去本此意旨所述筆觸及用筆二章即骨法用筆是四畫類及簡

韻去動應寫作繪畫之目的蜜非法則第二項以下則但為方法用故此求達至

笑以以今日眼光論之作殊合科學之理惟此意六法應作五法去第一項氣

位置六曰傳移模寫自謝赫創此六法故學者僉以宗出于得本來莫之廢

六法之道曰氣韻生動二曰骨法用筆三曰應物象形四曰隨類傳彩五曰經營

學者不易領悟求空像目理法狀默呈序呈以屬律袋者究此謝赫之六法中

吾國畫法代名作者惟多不脫文人積習好高務遠故弄玄虛以詞害意致使

淵求免顧此失彼不能舊及西學者雅意殷殷將何以應之學山緣作此去

去斫到美先坐二次至今十年修乎品跡所之從學者眾惟因時間短促地域遠

六壺亦洗筆之用瓷製鐵製均可

之碟亦備二三隻為調色調墨之用

稍粗而不光滑者俱可作練習之用

攀希在國外一切水彩畫布或色布俱屬此類店性與絹布相同擇宜質

之希亦生熟二種生者較宜希多韻味惟性不易畫 水多助番少助枯飛希亦

昭綡白粉石青石綠為硯賀不透明

三色余用之色極屬簡單如紅黄青珠白粉石青石綠兩己紅黄青珠屬透

二墨須用硯畫臨时磨而用之不可用墨汁盖洋而不化毫無韻味

者凡二三枝

背景兩用此上三種除排筆另一枝已夠應用 惟甲乙兩種應備大小不同

一筆大約亦分三種甲筆毛尖而不化開亦去為畫凡拘勒之作以及小点細查俱

可用此乙筆毛化開亦没骨畫之粗枝大葉俱可用此丙排筆或稱調筆多屬

第二章　用具

一反三覆皆径臨役日習運之皆耳

今照歷年所出種驗引述去店要之法助文字力未簡易棟圆務求簡多卟能举

畫以墨為主以色為輔色之不可奪墨猶賓之不可躐主也苟非成惜墨如金王

第三章　用墨

氣韻蓋此昭代李潤先所說者特述之屬學者參考

機蹶費五曰活筆筆勢飛遠乍徐還疾候聚忽散六曰潤筆含滋蘊致生

處昭三曰老筆如蒼藤古柏峻石屈鐵玉坼罐走四曰勁筆如強弓巨弩鏃

筆法大致不外此類一曰神筆縱橫妙理變化莫測二曰清筆簡俊縈潔疏諮

助剝也

心用筆膽大又曰磨墨如病夫執筆如壯士能如是則意在筆先筆不到而意

宜徐應詳如者慮待用筆時助元膽大者半不能且所顧慮所詎審察宜細

用筆之法須呂輕重疾徐未動筆前何處宜拈何處宜重何處宜疾何處

或筆鋤小者力用指力若線條長或筆觸大者非用腕力不可

以中峯屬抄作畫用腕力時助筆須握緊若用指力則筆須放鬆線條短

印側峯此稱方筆大概平兩扁之物体以用側峯較易表白至于圓而渾者助

第二章　用筆

當照用筆之道須先知執筆古時用直卯中峯此稱圓筆古時用斜

帝前不能在調色碟調勻召助成某一混合色不能顯出數色美的青興

着帝時能現出種不同之色且極目繄蘁痕跡唯主一疾須混注惡即未着

以工不同之色此與用墨相異其空法將筆先調某色次加另乙色或又乙色助筆

灌筆根傷淡或先調色次調水助筆端る淡筆根為灌乙褛色即乙筆用三種

之法甞異懂洽用墨之法自然能知用色之道即乙先調水次調色助筆端為

用色之法有今單色褛色二種甲單色即乙筆蠟僅用乙種色敕此與用墨

第の章　用色之法

此次調勻筆毛次加墨于筆端助灌淡自然融洽没骨花卉多用此法

先用淡墨積至可觀處役用灌墨分出畦径及遠近乙灌淡同时并用即先

先用灌墨作針次以淡墨水凍之必增窗厚或先用淡墨次加灌墨乃作出

至于温筆よ今二種畫法甲灌淡分別兩用即先用灌墨次加淡墨乃留松針

所以神觧不浮動古文家荒卒蒼茅三氣皆役乾筆敕擦中得束不可不知

多種不同之現象用墨須另乾弓瀹乌灌弓淡迂人作畫弓温弓灌弓淡兩螢乾

古人云墨分五色墨暢墨色何能今為五色蓋言乙灌淡瀹之不同故有仍

洽淡墨薄成畫惜者骨疏秀澹者氣碌碌學者須明惜墨澹墨の字

中國畫對于線條極關重要勾勒畫固純屬線條之組織即沒骨畫亦由

第六章　筆觸（即線條）

故畫初學者應先從勾勒入手待習相當技能再學沒骨

點畫成物形一部畫中亦以部分用勾勒部分用沒骨以亡為意趣畫者

曰描故曰描係勾勒之一種至于沒骨畫不用線條勾輪廓直接用墨水或色

勾物形之輪廓再加色彩或水墨點只僅用線條勾而不加墨水或彩色點則稱

成畫之方法而言勾勒與沒骨二種前詔勾勒亦稱雙勾即用線條先

意畫任意揮寫不拘細謹唐吳道子寫嘉陵江一日而成即寫意畫也今

一工筆畫上謹七細唐李思訓寫嘉陵江五日一山五日一水即工筆畫也二寫

也若根據題材而言則呂人物走獸山水花鳥等之繪像而言則呂

畫之種類呂多種不同之分法若根據材料而言則呂油畫水彩色粉墨水

第五章　畫之種類

助呆板興趣

另紅而非混合于金于用粉亦應多用墨之法即須呈濃呈淡切忌平塗若

紅調助成紫的混合色若先調青役僅于筆端加紅助至結果部分屬青部分

之為而配以他畫之花木或摹甲作之木移置于乙作之山石上而另成一畫

照他人作品摹寫部分而捨去餘或取數畫之長而配為一例或取此畫

學論章法題材色彩者。二依照他人作品摹寫之不改加變二部分臨摹即

摹臨之俾能領悟種三畫法上之要則臨摹之道分三種一完全臨摹

他人所作模寫之初學者對于作畫未到門徑不知如何著手故將名人作品

臨摹三字與寫生對之曰寫生係寫宇宙間之物象非臨他人作品臨摹則將

第七章　臨摹

宜顧慮形態尚須注意線條

答曰若能不失形態且線條本身六覺自然二者兼備則寫上業若則與

曲不相似而線條本身具另美之價值然助注重形態郎抑注重線條郎

因之物形曲似而線條失却自然之時不顧形態而任意擇寫結果形態

要為何必姬于字另一問題即呈時顧慮物形對于線條不能任意擇留

供依運用粗細圓秉名種之線條而表現不同之現象由此可知線條之重

丁頭鼠尾等之派語人物六八描而作山水另所語荅劈皴麻披皴乱柴皴等

短線或翹線配合而成古代作人物之衣褶另十八種不同之描法曰流水行雲

俱佳千里之水不俱秀山叢之花不俱美散文之木不俱雅月是二石互觀

必人是二嶧圓石對稱架勤作時不能同樣姿態三選擇得宜萬重之山不

宜勻稱作二樣不能高下一樣作三石忌大小相同必須錯落才徵不使呆板

審務求疎密古人云密不透風疎可容馬實佈局要得之法二不

目是取其損美觀章法姿化覺寬窄要疎密二須且疎密實中求疎密

章法即佈局於構圖繪畫上極關緊要章法猶人之姿態姿態不佳曲眉

第八章　章法

綠芭蕉與紅蜻蜓者由此始也可悟臨摹之道矣

故我曰海非作一大幅荷葉栗而用一点紅花者即我此作即取法於之改作

蜻蜓次日將該畫示諸生異謂其生曰我此畫係臨池之作品其生范然不解其

空中僅是含苞將放之紅花一朵疎忽生迦余印取意作一綠芭蕉栗上樓一紅

法將作樹木此用筆之臨摹也記余昔年執教時見某生作一大幅荷葉栗寫綠琳璃

空用焦墨方法而作山水尖用墨之臨摹也他人用傷筆寫岩山水我模空傷筆之

寫梅花我模空章法而改作桃李章法之臨摹也他人以焦墨寫花木我則模

三畫法臨摹以上三兩種臨摹拳俱足取衆之所嗜至于畫法臨摹拳助否例如他人

渲染之筆不用排筆以渲染時須勻稱不可露筆痕
上只宜用線條表現之吾筆而用材料若不以渲染列出何必捨易就難。
多用背景而多作渲染蓋所作多係絹本不以渲染即以雲與水在宣紙

吾國之畫多不用渲染非不欲用蓋宣紙不宜于渲染也須唐宋出畫

第十章　渲染

須技秀梢一不慎則弱点畢露故覺雜讀甚以宣紙雜而不敢試
化之道了唯紫易簡難紫則由勻敗筆難易隱藏簡則一点一劃俱
意多趣味之條鈔而册去宣甚意義甚趣味者這就難于簡
狐廻由此可見古人對于筆墨極注意于簡化此非謂畫賤應取宣多
此唐張彥遠日夫畫特忌形貌釆章歷三具足古謹長細而外宣巧密所以
國畫此要在平用筆之貴三平簡潔素成情畫的金言若不多貴筆墨

第九章　簡化

詳察繁雜之事物取宣粗華捨宣精粗配合于適宜之宣
此右觀又名被同是一鳥置于此宣屬宜放于彼宣助召吾人須以銳利眼光

Chapter 1

TRADITIONAL METHODS AND TECHNIQUES

In a country with ancient traditions, such as China, true originality must be built upon the methods and attainments of the past. There is perhaps no better way to open a discussion of Chinese painting than to refer to the *Hsieh Ho Liu Fa*, the Six Canons of Hsieh Ho. During the Northern Ch'i Dynasty this poet and critic formulated a set of principles governing the objectives and techniques of painting, and over the fourteen centuries which have followed, his Six Canons of Painting have been widely accepted. The Liu Fa, in the opinion of the Chinese masters, do not standardize the styles of scholarly painters, but offer a means of heightening and crystallizing their individuality. With a discerning and discriminating mind, an artist's technical skill must evolve to a high level before he is truly ready for self-expression. Then the brush becomes the medium by which he can interpret and express his inner feeling.

I shall attempt to condense and restate the Six Canons of Hsieh Ho in such a manner as to make them readily comprehensible. In the list that follows, it will be seen that the first canon has to do with the state of mind of the painter. The other five deal largely with methods and techniques. Each canon is in two parts.

Canon 1. The spirit of painting (Ch'i-yun), and rhythmic vitality (Sheng-tung).

Canon 2. Natural form and structure (Ku-fa), and the brush techniques employed (Yung-pi).

Canon 3. Depiction of a subject according to its nature (Ying-wu), and the brush and ink techniques employed (Hsiang-hsing).

Canon 4. Color (Sui-lei), and its application (Fu-ts'ai).

Canon 5. Composition (Ching-ying), and the selection of subjects (Wei-ch'i).

Canon 6. Study of classic paintings (Chuan-mo), and the copying of ancient masterpieces (I-hsieh).

The chapters that follow contain discussions of all these principles and procedures, but not always in the order of the canons listed. Rather than expound the canons, I have followed them in only a general way, setting forth simple outlines as a primary text for the art student. These may also supply information for those concerned only with art appreciation.

The first canon, rhythmic vitality, is abstract, and is regarded as the most essential feature in a work of art. It is difficult to define its import, because it is directed toward the spirit of the onlooker rather than toward his intellect. It may be said that its expression is a spontaneous outflow of the painter's own spirit. The painting reveals an artist's innermost feelings toward the forces that enliven every form in nature. Rhythmic vitality may be defined as the spirit existing in the rhythm of the universe. Through its use the artist tries to express the creative essence, the soul, and not the outward form.

We must bear in mind that a work of art is creative rather than imitative. Deft skill and sure technique, as covered by the other five canons, will help the artist to attain his purpose, in creating a painting that gives the obvious surface meaning together with a profound inner message. Since he desires to express the essential essence of his subject through its outward form, the Chinese artist must always have its rhythmic vitality uppermost in his thoughts. His painting will have living beauty if it arouses emotion in the spectator, who thus becomes a collaborator.

Only when a student has become familiar with all six canons will he sense the intimate relationship between the rhythmic vitality that flows through all forms of nature and the living beauty of his creation. A good painting must always have this quality of creative beauty, revealing the spirituality of the painter as well as his profound mastery of the brush. This canon is closely related to the beholder, because discernment is dependent upon both his aesthetic and his imaginative capabilities. Traditionally, the Chinese artist is a scholar, a self-effacing man of culture, not a person concerned merely with pictorial representation. Thoroughly conversant with the history and traditions of his country, well versed in its poetry and other literature, he uses painting as the medium for expressing his awareness of all that is beautiful in the world around him.

It may be well to state at this point that I have no intention of writing an erudite commentary on the historical development of Chinese art, or the problems which have arisen during past centuries. What I am trying to say comes from my long years of experience; I have confined myself to what I consider essentials, and shall augment the text with appropriate illustrations of my work. It is my earnest wish that the reader may learn the principles of Chinese painting, and be enabled to improve his work and increase his enjoyment of it, in whatever school he has been trained.

Chapter 2

PAINTING MATERIALS

Essential tools and equipment needed for painting in the Chinese manner are few: brushes, ink and inkstone, water colors, paper, containers for paint and water.

Brushes. Three kinds of brushes are generally used:

A stiff brush with a sharp point, made from deer, horse, or wolf hair, is used for calligraphy as well as painting. Such brushes come in three bristle sizes—long, medium, and short—and all will prove useful for outline work and for thin, fine lines and dots. To prepare this brush for initial use, dip the bristle in water to half its length only; then, holding the handle horizontally, gently loosen the tip by a slight downward pressure.

A soft brush, without a sharp point, made from goat, rabbit, or sable hair, is used for freehand work such as executing heavy branches, large leaves, and flower petals, and for applying ink or color. The entire bristle is softened before use.

A wide, soft brush with no point is used for background work or washes. One of these is sufficient unless the artist becomes involved with many large paintings.

Brush handles are always made of bamboo, as shown in the photographs on page 23. Brush prices range widely, depending on quality. The Chinese brush is a subtle and plastic instrument, extremely versatile and susceptible of an almost infinite variety of strokes. A skillful artist can manipulate it to produce lines sharp and concise, broad and quivering, light or dark, all according to the requirements of the subject. The pigment may be spread to strong strokes or thinned to delicate shades at his pleasure. Without breaking his stroke, he may change from a broad to a narrow line, from an irregular mass to a smooth and slender shading, and he may quicken or reduce his speed at will.

The ink and inkstone. Chinese artists mix their own ink. Prepared ink which comes in bottles should never be used, for it does not express fine shadings. Ink is prepared for use by grinding pigment from a Chinese black ink-stick or block. The ink-stick is made by impregnating gum with soot from pine smoke. Place a few drops of water on an inkstone and grind the ink-stick against it. Two or three hundred turns of the hand, depending on the pressure, will make enough for immediate use. Fresh ink should be made at the beginning of each day's work.

The inkstone is flat and may be carved in various shapes, and with decorative patterns. Many beautiful ones have been made from early Chinese history, and these are precious to the collector. The novice, however, may use a simple inkstone which is not expensive. One of good quality should be washed clean after use to preserve its fine surface.

Water colors. The following pigments are used: red, yellow, blue, orange, white, stone blue, and stone green. Transparent colors are red, yellow, blue, and orange. Opaque colors are white, stone blue, and stone green.

Chinese water colors are made in either pellet or powder form. Their dyes are derived from vegetable juices in some cases: yellow from the bark and sap of rattan, blue from indigo. Black comes from the soot of pine mixed with oil or gum. Some colors are obtained entirely from minerals: red from cinnabar and coral, blue from lapis lazuli, yellow from orpiment, white from white lead (poisonous) or burnt oyster shells. Chinese painters of long ago ground small white pearls for their white powder. All colors except yellow have an addition of animal glue which imparts a strong, characteristic odor.

These pigments may be used if the artist desires, but water colors made by Western manufacturers are wholly adequate.

Paper. Non-absorbent paper with a hard finish, treated with alum, is best suited for slow, detailed work. If Chinese paper is not at hand, use any water-color paper available at art-supply stores.

Absorbent paper, commonly called rice paper though made from cotton, has a fine, soft texture. It takes much practice and skill to paint on such a surface. If too much water remains on the brush, the ink or water color will spread when applied, making it difficult to draw the shape desired. On the other hand, if the brush is too dry, completing a stroke is difficult if not impossible. Only after experimenting with his brush and mastering the technique can a student learn to apply quick brush strokes on absorbent paper, with the spontaneity and suppleness of line so characteristic of Chinese painting. All strokes must be made rapidly and without hesitation, from beginning to end. The impression of spontaneity given by Chinese art is effected by the rapidity of the artist's brush strokes.

The earliest Chinese painting, before the invention of paper, was done on silk. Modern artists still paint on silk occasionally, but paper, because it is less porous, is better suited to either delicate or strong brush strokes. In China drawing paper is made from hemp, mulberry, and bamboo, as well as cotton.

Containers. Three or four small white plates will serve for mixing and testing pigments. They should be carefully washed after each use, so that colors are always clean. Any vessel that holds water can be used for washing brushes.

All the materials enumerated are available at Chinese shops dealing in paper and stationery items, and are usually found in large American cities.

Chapter 3

HOW TO HANDLE THE BRUSH

In Chinese painting the paper is laid on a flat surface at table level. Sit with good posture in a straight-backed chair. After preparing your ink and colors, it will be helpful to "play" with your brushes before you begin to think about painting. This preparatory exercise of the hand may lead the artist into a proper mood.

Hold the handle of the brush a little below the center. Place it between the thumb and first finger, resting the lower part on the nail of the third finger. The second finger rests on the handle just below the first. The thumb braces the handle.

The brush may be held upright, perpendicular to the paper when making dots and curved or straight lines. In this position the brush should be held firmly.

For making side-strokes, rectangular lines, and shallow, flat figures, hold the brush loosely in horizontal position, with the palm of the hand turned toward the body. The stroke is made with pressure on the whole brush, from point to base.

Finger movements are used to manipulate the brush when making short lines, small points, and dots. The arm directs the brush in making long lines and heavy strokes. When painting a large picture, the artist should stand and lean over the table. This position enables him to make free movements of the arm and hand, and permits the whole body to work in coordination. Depending upon the subject, strokes

Traditional ways of holding the brush.

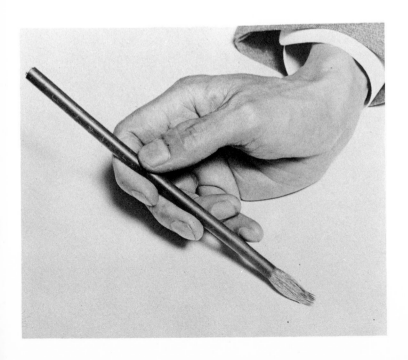

are made either light or heavy, either fast or slow. The technique should be decided upon in advance, so that the artist may proceed with confidence.

There is a Chinese saying, "In planning be careful and deliberate, but when the brush is in hand show courage and self-confidence." Another offers further advice: "In grinding ink use slow, long-drawn-out movements, such as a weary person might employ in his labor; but when holding the brush, work as if you were a courageous hero." If the artist is to follow this advice and proceed in this manner, he must have planned the composition well in advance.

Painting 1. Lotus. To paint the stems, veins, and grass, a pointed brush was used. This was held in a vertical position. A larger brush, with the bristle fanned out, was used to paint the leaves and for this area the whole arm was moved. For the center of the flower and the small markings on the stems, a small brush and only finger and wrist movements were required.

24

照李閒先所謀之老筆，以蒼籐古柏峻石屈鐵玉圻走蟪，此畫約畧似之。

此老梅須用中鋒，除点苔心可以用指力外，宜徐俱須用腕力。

Painting 2. Plum Blossoms. The strokes depicting the tree trunk and branches were done in a vigorous fashion to express strength and virility. The blossoms and birds add decorative touches of color.

Since Chinese painting and calligraphy are sister arts, the Chinese scholar who paints is almost always an accomplished calligrapher. Our written language uses ideograms to express ideas not only accurately but artistically, and for this reason the works of our great calligraphers have been treasured throughout Chinese history.

Through assiduous study and long practice, the hand of the artist should acquire such facility in handling the brush that his mind and hand are left wholly free to express his thoughts. This is of the utmost importance, for strength or feebleness plainly shows in the stroke. Only after rigorous training may he gain firm and balanced control of the brush. He should take such exercises as these: press and lift, push and pull, turn and twist, dash and sweep.

即先將筆調水次醮墨于筆端助筆端屬濃筆根屬淡

雞之腹部腿部及尾部以及錦葵之葉俱示用墨濃淡同時幷用之法

Painting 3. Rooster and Hollyhock. This illustration demonstrates the use of light and dark ink simultaneously. The technique is to be seen on the feathers of the breast, legs, and tail of the cock, and also on the leaves of the hollyhock. After the bristle was charged with water, just the point was dipped in ink, so that the stroke started out dark and became lighter as the whole of the bristle was pressed down.

26

Chapter 4

PAINTING WITH BLACK INK

Great significance has been attached to ink painting in China for centuries. It reached its height during the Sung Dynasty (960 to 1279), and is still a major method of artistic expression.

There are five shadings of black ink, involving gradations of depth from jet black to light gray. These are dependent upon the amount of water carried on the brush, as follows:

Heavy black. To obtain this value a dry brush is dipped in the ink.

Strong black. A wet brush with the water squeezed out is dipped in the ink.

Medium black. Place a small amount of ink on a dish and add a few drops of water.

Light black (gray). Use approximately half water and half ink.

Very light black (light gray). Use mostly water with a few drops of ink.

These gradations are used to show vitality, perspective, and spontaneity in a painting. Beauty of line can be expressed by their effective use. It requires great skill and good judgment on the part of the artist to produce the various ink values and tone qualities. Ancient scholars have felt that these gradations suggest all variations of color. Only a fine artist can express mellowness, richness, and softness in black ink.

There are two methods of using ink on a wet brush:

Heavy black and light black may be applied separately, to show dark and light objects. (*See painting* 6.)

They may be applied simultaneously. Dip the brush first in water and then in thick, black ink. Upon application the brush stroke is dark at first, and becomes progressively lighter. Or the stroke thus applied may show an interesting blending of light and dark throughout. (*See paintings* 3, 4, 5, 7.)

A wet brush with light or dark ink is comparatively easy to manipulate, but a student may often have trouble with a dry brush at first. The brush should be dipped into ink, most of which is then removed by rubbing on a blotter or scrap paper. Strokes executed with a brush prepared in this manner impart a mottled effect; they give a lifelike quality and spontaneous simplicity to a painting. A partially dried brush may leave parts of the stroke broken or open, but the continuity of idea is there. Differences in texture and shading, and the subtle nuances of ink tones, produce a most pleasing effect. Many old masters enjoyed painting in this manner.

Sometimes the outline of a composition is made with brush strokes using black ink, and colors are added as accents. Ink is often used sparingly in the outline, and darker strokes are added for natural contrasts. (*See painting* 27.) During the T'ang Dynasty Li Cheng used ink so sparingly that it was said that he saved it as if it were gold. His aim was the utmost restraint and simplicity. Wang Chieh, another artist of that time, used ink generously, and his work looks as though he had poured it on. He did this to show greatness, boldness, and character. The painter should understand these two points of approach. He will then know when it is appropriate to use ink profusely, and when he should be economical with it.

此二圖俱用墨水作成。先將筆調水次醮墨在碟內畧調。不可逗多。方能部分之部分。屬濃部分而不淡。且融洽調和。不露迹痕。若于碟內多調。則緣成淡墨。以濃

Paintings 4 and 5. Bird and Butterfly; Banana Palms. Here again dark and light ink have been used in combination. The entire bristle was dipped in water, and then just the tip was lightly touched in ink to produce the monochromatic shadings.

頸、尾部先点睛、補迄、此濃淡分別而用之法。

畫鶴助、先用淡墨拘定身、次以濃墨畫頭

三象、次以濃墨作松針、再以淡墨染之。

以淡墨写松幹、再用枯筆擦之、俾顯蒼莽

Painting 6. "Longevity." A light ink (black ink mixed with water) was used to outline the trunk and branches. Then a dry brush was applied for darker shadings. The needles of the pine tree were done in the strongest black. In painting each crane, light ink outlined the body and dark ink was used for the neck, tail, and legs. This is an example of the use of light and dark ink separately.

Painting 7. Bamboo. To paint the branches the brush was dipped in light ink, then the bristle was fanned out and dipped first on its left side and then on its right in a little darker ink. The illustration demonstrates the use of light and dark ink in combination.

因淨之故、尖上濃淡同時弁用之法。

則筆毛之二边為濃、中為淡、現出

用手指將筆毛揑扁、左右離濃墨、

写竹幹先將筆調淡墨、覚飽和皮。

白粉亦何常不可合為五色耶？寧在另滾另淡耳。

齊剪之圖案何異。那能生動。學者應知用粉之道，要如用墨之法。墨分五色，

用白粉須另滾另淡，雞身背部，及翼宜滾。腹部腿部須較淡另紫滾淡助興

Painting 8. Taro and White Hen. The bird in this illustration demonstrates a happy use of white pigment. Heavy white was placed on the back and wings of the hen, and lighter white on the other parts. Touches of grayed white were applied simultaneously to produce fluffy feathers.

Chapter 5

PAINTING WITH COLOR

Chinese painting is known for its richness in the use of soft colors, which tend to subordinate all the elements of a picture into a harmonious whole. This is in keeping with the spiritual values desired by the Chinese. Their urge for a calm and tranquil spirit is satisfied by the quality of color employed by the old masters, who often indulged in color abstractions, a rendering of self-tones of a single color.

The student must learn the essentials of color mixing, color matching, and color application, both in producing monochromatic effects and in the use of many colors. Monochromatic painting with color follows the same technique that has been described for the use of black ink, on pages 27 and 28. Wet the brush in water and dip just its tip in color. On paper the first part of the stroke will show a deep color tone, with the lightest color at the base of the stroke, and with various shadings in between. This procedure can be reversed by charging the whole brush with color, then dipping its point in water. The ensuing brush stroke will show color in lighter tone at the beginning, gradually deepening with greater brilliance at the base. Subtle and exquisite nuances may be produced in this manner.

In the past, Chinese painters have not made much use of white, because they thought of it as a flat color with few nuances. However, highly effective results can be obtained by using white paint on off-white or tinted papers. I have enjoyed painting with white, and have taught many students the following technique. Use white paint as you would black ink; in other words, strive for variations in tone, making some parts of the stroke heavy, other parts light. Do not apply it in an even tone (just one shade of white), or the stroke will turn out to be stiff and flat. The intensity of white will vary according to the wetness or dryness of the brush. (*See paintings* 8, 11.)

Two or more colors can be used on the same brush and can be applied to the paper in a single stroke. Dip the damp brush lightly in one color, then in another, and even in a third or fourth if you wish. Moving over the surface, the colors may be mixed on the brush as you paint, and all of them will be brought out and blended. This mixing of colors will produce new tones and shades without distinguishing lines between them, and often the most intricate and exquisite shadings will be produced. It must be emphasized that the paints are not to be mixed in the dish beforehand if this effect is desired. But if the artist dips his brush in blue, and then in red, one portion of the brush stroke will be blue and another red, with a soft blending of both colors as well. The effect of these subtle transitional hues of red-violet, violet, and violet-blue can be attained only by the most skillful handling of the brush. (*See paintings* 9, 10, 13, 19.)

There is still another method of using two colors simultaneously which may prove effective. If you use a brush with a broad tip, with a different color on each side, the strokes will produce parallel lines which greatly accentuate the form and accent of an object. (*See painting* 7.) Wise choice of contrasting colors is obviously required for this technique, as well as brush mastery.

In painting the feathers of birds, I have always tried to produce a fluffy and soft effect. After some experimentation I have found that the following procedure produces the desired texture. Place a little white pigment in a dish, add a dash of black ink, and mix them only partially, never thoroughly. Use of the half-mixed white and black produce luminous grayish tones which makes the feathers seem vibrantly alive. (*See painting* 8.)

Opposite: Painting 9. Taro and Wisteria. The wisteria (right) is in shades of purple, made with a mixture of red and blue water color. A clean brush was charged with white water color; then the point was dipped in the purple and brushed onto the paper. For the leaf (left), a clean brush was charged with blue-green pigment, and just the point dipped in red. The stem was painted starting at the top and moving toward the bottom, with the result that the upper part came out mostly red, the lower part mostly blue-green. The stroke was started with a fine, light touch, which gradually broadened into a heavier line at the bottom.

不能在碟內調勻各列成為混合色矣。
青末雖紅。所當注意者所用二色或三色，
次雖青三光調紅次雖墨。光調黃次雖
種不同之象。一光調黃次雖紅。二光調黃，
所作之業用各種不同之色遂現出矣。

Opposite: Painting 10. Leaves. These are four practice plates showing the combination of different colors in one stroke:

1. The bristle was first charged in yellow, then the point was dipped in red.
2. The brush was dipped in yellow and the point in blue.
3. The brush was dipped in red and just the tip in black ink.
4. The brush was first dipped in yellow, then in blue, and lastly just the tip in red.

For this technique it is most important not to mix the colors beforehand. If the brush is dipped into the colors separately, the colors will arrange themselves on the paper in blends and textures as the brush stroke is applied.

灌，下部為青。上部細下部粗美。

如黃）次蘸紅色自上而下由輕而重，則上部為

帝前二色不調匀，畫法先將筆調青（可是

筆根為白。至于左圖，先幹點紅青二色唯着

再以他筆調紫筆端蘸紫色贴筆端蘸紫，

右圖紫藤係紅青二色調匀成為紫的混合色。

没骨畫。

為宜。若用白粉，最好用線條拘出之，不能作白粉之加墨水始能顯出陰陽向背，而用之粉以召背景毛羽必骨參用，此幅孔崔之毛，雲灰色部分蓋墨白粉與墨水二者相反不能混合唯巨时作翎毛之

Painting 11. Peacock. White pigment and black ink are opposites, and, while old Chinese masters did not mix the two in the manner shown here, the combination may, nevertheless, be most effective. A tinted paper is recommended, for white pigment does not of course show up well on a pure white background.

Opposite: Painting 13. Cinerarias. These flowers were painted with a brush dipped first in white pigment, then in blue, and next in red at the tip. The cineraria leaves were painted in a combination of brown, yellow, and blue pigments combined on the brush. Darker parts of the leaves have more blue, while the lighter have more brown and yellow.

34

于雪工因不透照，故仍以題照。
墨水寫成，次如綠色染之，待乾乃再加石青
石青石綠俱礦質不透照，此幅之樹光用

Painting 12. Cypress Trees. Here the trees are accented with stone blue, an opaque mineral paint. They were first outlined in light black ink; then when this was thoroughly dry the blue was brushed in, in small firm strokes. The scene in the background was washed in first.

用青澱家則多用黃與硃。
墨之法必先與葉用青與黃異如硃濃墨多
端多青與紅故部分屬濃部分屬淡此與用
畫此花用白粉花青胭脂三色筆根多枝筆

中峰拘之。全畫俱須用腕力。墨論墨水或色彩，切須多用水分，方感淋漓老徹。此係沒骨畫也。芸花芸葉須用較大之筆，芸毛全部化開側峰作之。至于葉莖助用

Painting 14. Sunflowers. An example of the Mo Ku method of painting. The sunflowers and leaves were painted with a large brush held in a slanting position with its bristle -fanned out. For the veins of the leaves, the brush (slightly wetter) was held vertically, and arm movements were used.

Chapter 6

STYLES OF PAINTING

There are two basic techniques in Chinese painting, Kung Pi, which is stylized, and Hsieh-i, which the Chinese call the free-brush method. Paintings in the Kung Pi manner are characterized by great detail, and the work is done with slow, fine strokes of the brush. The famed T'ang Dynasty painter Li Ssu-hsun once painted a landscape called "Chialing Chiang" on which he worked for five days to complete the mountains, and as many more on the water. The result was a precise water color showing everything in great detail. (*See paintings* 23, 25.)

In direct contrast to the Kung Pi style, the Hsieh-i artist paints freely and boldly. He knows his subject well, and with the picture he wants to paint firmly established in his mind he executes it rapidly and with great apparent ease. Only essential details are shown, and the forms produced are full of spontaneity and life. (*See paintings* 24, 26.) In contrast to the meticulous and slow procedure of Li Ssu-hsun described above, another famous painter of the T'ang Dynasty, Wu Tao-tzu, took only one day to complete the same subject in the Hsieh-i style. According to the emperor who commissioned the two artists to portray the identical scene, both paintings were equally good. Hsieh-i may be said to be a free interpretation of nature. The artist must have a sure hand, and a memory trained to the highest point. He studies his subject, then paints from memory only what he considers the essential elements, using the fewest possible strokes. With complete mastery of his brush and his color technique, he will attain perfect coordination of mind and hand.

There are three other terms commonly encountered in discussions of Chinese painting techniques. These are Ke Le, Pai Miao, and Mo Ku. Ke Le involves drawing the outline of an object and then filling in the enclosed area with color. (*See paintings* 20, 27.) Pai Miao means drawing the outline without adding color. Mo Ku signifies a painting that has no outline work; literally translated from the Chinese, it means a "boneless" painting, but it is by no means as unattractive as this term sounds. The painter works directly with color or ink on his brush, without previously sketching an outline to follow. This method, which shows strength and elegance in the freehand strokes of the brush, requires a great deal of skill. In executing broad washes or masses, the painter concentrates on the essentials, a method diametrically opposed to the elaborate, detailed procedure followed in Ke Le or Pai Miao. (*See paintings* 14, 16, 18, 21, 22.)

Sometimes we find a combination of Ke Le and Mo Ku in one painting, and this can result in interesting contrasts. Often, too, we find that a beginner draws only the outline of an object, as a first step in learning. Later, when he is thoroughly familiar with the subject matter, he may paint it again freely, omitting the outline. Various combinations of brushwork, form, and color, all in one painting, produce fascinating results. Unity and variety, harmony and contrast, must always be borne in mind. (*See paintings* 15, 17.)

潔不宜繁雜。
先用淡墨鈎輪廓，次用黃色染之。所鈎數筆意簡
全身作成，再以濃墨加尾，添翼毛玉子小雞勁多鈎勒。
母雞居沒骨畫用化開之筆，自頭及身由濃及淡待

Painting 15. Mother Hen. An example combining the Mo Ku and
Ke Le techniques. The hen was painted in Mo Ku style with a bristle
brush fully fanned out. Working from head to body, dark to light
gradations of ink were applied. Dark ink was then added on the
wings and tail. The baby chicks represent Ke Le or outline painting.
Here light ink was used to draw the simple outline, and color applied
later in the enclosed areas.

雞畫法不同。
沒骨畫與上圖之小
此三小雞並無輪廓係

Painting 16. Baby Chicks. A Mo Ku painting. No outline
was drawn in this case. Comparison with the young birds
in painting 15 shows the wide difference in techniques.

雞屬沒骨寫畫法如前所述者玉于背份之花刻為沒骨七謹七細
以形近言雖為寫意畫花則工筆畫也

Painting 17. Hen and Bouvardias. Here the same technique was
employed as for the hen in painting 15. The background flowers were
first executed in outline. The detailed work on them, and the freehand style employed for the bird, shows the Kung Pi and Hsieh-i
techniques in combination.

Painting 18. Pink Roses. The petals in this Mo Ku painting were made with pink; when the paint was thoroughly dry, the light and dark accents were added in white and red.

Painting 19. Rose. Here the flower was painted with a brush dipped first in light green, then in red. The colors blended on the paper and ended in mostly green on the lower petal. Blue and yellow were combined for the leaves, with more blue used for the darker leaves. The lighter hues were achieved by adding more water to the pigments. The young, tender leaves were painted with a touch of red and brown.

分嬌柔而加琳與紅色。

敷色不以同時并用之一例。至于畫葉不用花青與藤黃，澹勾多加花青淡勾多如水

以表明反轉之花瓣。又下圖之花將筆先調淡綠，再調紅色，故左下一花瓣畢呈綠色。此必

上下二圖之月季俱系没骨畫寫花時將筆調紅色作成花瓣，待色乾後再以白粉畢如教筆，

紫或綠自始至終用力應均勻粗細宜相同花不用淡墨鉤葉與幹則用濃墨此月季係鉤勒法不用筆毛尖而不全部化開者以狼毫為佳蓋枝挺硬鉤勒時筆須握

Painting 20. Roses. Painted in the Ke Le technique. A brush with a stiff point was held firmly, and the same pressure on finger movements was applied from beginning to end. Light ink was used for the flowers and darker ink for the leaves and stems.

41

故不忽没骨之難也。
必須逼真，不能更改，拘勒畫可先作稿本任意更改，待確定後，印依稿描畫之
上下二圖俱爲没骨畫没骨雖不君拘勒之貴時亦較多種畫蓋每一筆觸

Paintings 21 and 22. Crabapple Blossoms; Grapes and Bluebird. Two paintings in the Mo Ku technique.

右圖之牡丹屬沒骨法稱寫意畫。左圖屬鈎勒法稱工筆畫。空花用淡墨鈎
出景則用較濃墨，幹亦灸濃，待鈎略乾再看加種之色。

Paintings 23 and 24. Peonies. The flower on the right was done in the Mo Ku
and Hsieh-i style, and the one on the left in the Ke Le and Kung Pi technique.

43

兩批枇杷則屬沒骨，左者一切俱係勾勒。

二者俱係鸚鵡屬題材，惟右者係寫意畫，左者屬工筆畫，右者之鸚鵡為勾勒。

Paintings 25 and 26. Parrots. The picture on the right was executed in the Mo Ku and Hsieh-i technique, and the one on the left in the Ke Le and detailed Kung Pi style.

Painting 27. Chinese Lilies. A monochromatic study, painted in the Ke Le method. The outlines of the flowers were drawn in light ink, the centers in dark ink, as were the outline of the leaves. Next, lighter ink was brushed on to fill the enclosed areas of the leaves and petals. The entire painting was done in shades of gray from light to dark.

出陰陽向背不如顏色豫白描畫係拘勒之一種
此拘勒之水仙用淡墨拘花用濃墨拘葉及點花心拘好以黑用淡墨水染之以令

故下圖助用細線纏繞而成為工整。惟用剛勁之線條，仍不露柔弱之態。上下二圖用所用之筆觸不同，呈現象顏異。上圖係用大筆粗線任意揮寫，氣勢豪。

Paintings 28 and 29. Lofty Mountains; Babbling Brook. Two paintings illustrating different kinds of strokes. The one above, painted with the free-brush technique, has spontaneity and strength; the one below, executed slowly and meticulously, is less spontaneous, yet shows virility of line.

46

Chapter 7

THE IMPORTANCE OF LINE

A line or brush stroke may be long and thin or short and wide; even a dot may be considered a short line. Lines, either straight or curving, reproduce the shapes of all of the objects an artist wishes to paint. His skill is judged largely by the combination of suppleness and firmness that is indicated by his brush strokes. A painting of merit shows brushwork which has softness and harmony and at the same time gives the appearance of virility. Strokes which appear delicate may, paradoxically, exhibit great strength. More than any other element, the brush stroke embodies the technique of Chinese art. (*See painting* 29.)

As mentioned earlier, Ke Le paintings represent pure outline drawing, and are therefore fundamentally linear in character. They depend entirely upon the beauty of the stroke to attain the rhythm for which they are noted. Line brings out the contour to produce the illusion of perfect modeling. The thickness or thinness of the line depends on the pressure of the hand. In his free and eloquent brush strokes the artist may exert all his strength, starting from the shoulder and coursing down through his fingers to the tip of his brush. He must have a sure hand, for every stroke shows on the porous paper or silk, and there is no way of correcting an error. The student should aim for form, balance, and strength of stroke. His work will attain sweep and rhythm as he learns the technique of changing the pressure on his brush, so that the ink may spread in broad masses or in delicately shaded lines without interrupting their flow.

Mo Ku painting, though it does not employ outline as the starting point of a composition, is nevertheless made up of narrow or wide lines of varying character. Here the firmness of the brush stroke plays an equally important part. (*See paintings,* 28, 31.) A fine, thin line, a jagged line, a thick, heavy line, a soft, light line—each produces an entirely different effect. The whole mood of the painting is set by the quality of its lines. (*See paintings* 30, 32, 33.)

One may get an idea of the importance of line in Chinese painting by citing the following example. If an artist should paint a flower with meticulous care, he would reproduce its form perfectly but would probably not be placing emphasis on beauty of stroke. The result might be an exact copy, but would possess little feeling of growth and originality; it would be stiff and lacking in grace. Conversely, an artist might have only the quality of stroke in his mind, and pay little attention to the structure of his subject; the beauty of his strokes would be there, but the likeness would be inadequate. If he must err in one direction or the other, perhaps it is better for the artist to concentrate on beautiful strokes which are in themselves elegant, fluid, pleasing to the eye, rather than to paint a picture which is accurate and dull. (*See paintings* 34, 35.) But his ideal purpose should be to produce a combination of animation and faithfulness to physical detail, a painting whose beautiful strokes combine to present a good likeness of the subject. Such strokes provide the flowing rhythm and suspended motion that suggest the movement and continuity of living things. Brush strokes light and dark, wet and dry, heavy and thin, curved and straight, all with varied spacing—these the artist may achieve through long practice until his work shows power, flexibility, gracefulness, and balance.

以表風勢至于小菊、細草、尤須呈動態、由右向左、沿能與樹枝不相衝突。
所作風樹純用粗細線條鈎勒而成、用筆須流利活潑、老幹固可挺直而細枝必須飄搖。

Painting 30. Windblown Trees. The windblown effect was obtained by the use of thin and heavy lines. The strokes were executed freely and quickly, giving a lifelike quality to the subject. The trunks, not affected by the blowing of the wind, were painted in their natural growing position. In keeping with the direction of the wind the grass and small chrysanthemums lean the same as the branches and leaves.

待胸已成竹，勇往直前，此謂之巨筆。礦機颳發時開光派語勁筆是也。

此松鷹，取其雄健家故之勢。凡作畫，未動筆前，應先考慮題材，應用何種筆觸。

Painting 31. Eagle. A study showing great virility of stroke. To achieve this, the artist must have decided not only on the subject but on the exact type of strokes to be employed. He can then paint with confidence and courage. Both these qualities are discernible in strokes of the painting.

49

Paintings 32 and 33. Old Pine; Orchids. A study in contrasts. In the first painting heavy dark colors and broken lines depict the age and strength of an
ancient cypress tree. In the painting of the two orchids, light strokes and
soft colors were used to show tenderness and delicacy.

何種筆調，
惟些之筆調才能顯出嬌嫩美麗之姿態，學者應懂體物之趣，詳察何種題材，應採
工圓之老樹係用古樸況着之筆調方能顯出蒼莽古老之氣象。下圖蘭花則用秀俊

與尤注意于形態豈實注意于線條。兩線條本身失却自由。下圖則任意揮寫，瓶盆形態由不及上圖之糟。而線條流利得多。上下二圖俱屬盆景，上圖因顧憲瓶盆之形態，對于線條不能任意揮寫，故形態由正確。

Paintings 34 and 35. "New Year Greetings"; Floral Arrangements. The first gives the actual appearance of the containers and their contents by means of meticulously executed strokes. In the second painting the objects, which are not as carefully painted, produce a more animated effect with greater originality.

51

此圖係取右面下圖之葡萄而配以右面上圖之小鳥擇畫中我所愛好者合而爲一能如是

出乎臨摹而已懂日佈局之道可以變化愛竄不受臨本之拘束矣

Paintings 36, 37, and 38. Grapes, Birds, and Blossoms. These three pictures show how subject matter can be combined. The birds in the painting above and the grapes in the painting below are brought together and rearranged in the composition at left.

52

Chapter 8

COPYING AS A METHOD OF LEARNING

From ancient times to the present, Chinese artists have copied old masterpieces as a way of learning techniques. In following this procedure the student should not merely be making mechanical imitations; he should be striving to understand the skills of the painters of these older works of art, and his efforts should produce re-creations of the originals, painted with thought and intelligence. After learning how the great masters have worked, the young artist must gain complete mastery of the brush before it will respond to the commands of his mind. He may then consider himself adequately equipped to create independently.

There are three ways by which a student can copy another artist's work while learning. He may reproduce the painting in entirety—strokes, composition, colors; this may be useful to the beginner. Or he might copy only a portion of the painting, after dividing the composition into its component parts. With added experience he may find it desirable to select parts of more than one painting, and combine them into a new and complete study. (*See paintings* 36, 37, 38, 39, 40, 41.) This step will help the beginner to learn more about composition. If at this stage of his development a young artist particularly admires the strokes or colors used in the painting of another, he may profitably copy them in his own work. As an example, let us suppose that trees are an important part of a finished painting, and that the strokes used in painting them are of interest to the amateur. By way of experimentation he may adapt these strokes to his painting of flowers, with highly satisfactory results. Or it may be a beautiful and unusual combination of colors which attracts his attention, and which he may introduce into his own studies to advantage.

This approach to the appreciation of the paintings of others may be helpful to the experienced artist as well as to the beginner. One of my students once submitted to me a study he had just finished. In it he had used several shades of green to paint large lotus leaves, and then for color contrast he had added a red bud of the lotus blossom. The color combination was so striking that I at once adapted it in a painting of my own showing banana trees. The lovely fringed leaves were painted in shades of green, and for contrast I added a red dragonfly. Next day I showed my painting to the student who had painted the lotus, saying, "You see, I have learned from you too. I have adapted your technique." The boy answered, "Why no, master, I have never painted banana leaves with a dragonfly." Whereupon I explained that I had not copied his composition, but had only borrowed his idea of color combination.

In actual fact an artist sees new subjects to paint in every museum or gallery he visits. The techniques, colors, themes used by others are constantly suggesting procedures that can be adapted to his own use. If he is also constantly studying nature with a discerning eye, and storing what he sees in his mind, he will be able to transform this wealth of material, together with his innermost feeling, into a painting filled with rhythm, spontaneity, and living beauty. The Chinese have this to say

由上圖脫胎而成者也。
下圖之山水，即採取上圖之岩石，如人物，分即以遠景之夕陽，驟視之似另是新意也。

Paintings 39 and 40. "Inspiration Point"; Sunset. Another illustration of "borrowing." At first glance the picture at the left appears to be quite different from the one above. However, closer examination shows that the rocks in the foreground are similar. The setting sun over distant mountains, and the figures and other foreground details, have been added to provide a new composition.

about an artist: "He must have read ten thousand volumes and he must have traveled ten thousand miles before he is capable of interpreting and expressing his own feeling." In discussing the background of an artist I have frequently drawn upon this analogy: the silkworm feeds upon mulberry leaves, and after due process of digestion changes this material into silk; in similar fashion, the artist calls from memory material absorbed through keen study of the world about him, and transposes his knowledge into the desired end result, a dynamic painting.

A word of caution regarding copying may be added for the student. In the end, every artist must find his own means of expression, however closely his style may follow that of a master or of a school of art. If copying and imitation are continued beyond his days of learning, he may become so dependent upon this crutch that his creative ability will slowly become devitalized. He must ever bear in mind that while technique may be learned from his ancestors, inspiration comes directly from nature. Other artists' paintings may inspire the serious student, and stimulate his imagination by revealing new methods. It may not be difficult to reproduce the art form of another's work, but to capture and transfer the spirit is another matter.

Painting 41. Summer. A third variation shows a change in the position of the rock and the figures. In addition, a waterfall takes the place of the background mountains and sunset.

臨本待乎相其枝幹，應自行用心取他人之一部，而另構新圖，為將來自行創造之基礎。

畏峰一二，成例耳，學者由此而悟，何臨摹古人，在初學作畫時，未乃門徑，固不能不一臨，

此圖又連由39及40兩圖畫加變化而成，夕陽改為飛瀑，而人物則由右移為左，另成一畫，此不足

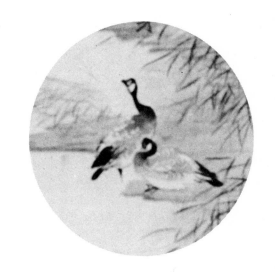

此數畫皆由の六圖中採取而成由此可照構圖之道全在學者慧心目用耳。

Paintings 42, 43, 44, 45, and 46. Geese. Components of the painting on the facing page are reproduced here as separate studies. These units may remain as complete pictures in themselves or they may be recombined to produce new compositions.

亂苔章突。

以一枝言若枝葉過繁可除去部分總之自然間形疏色濃由自己選擇及安排否則雜

佈濃淡不應高低相勻在一叢之花內取雲二三枝或三の枝最多選至乎意趣者而捨至源印

此六圖俱係同樣小菊之題材當論繪畫或按排盆景均須乎疏乎密錯落乎微不能全希

Chapter 9

COMPOSITION

Composition involves bringing together the various elements of a subject and placing them in a pleasing arrangement; it is the structure or framework upon which a work of art is built. Harmonious relationships of the component parts create the desired result, a sense of unity. There must be balance and harmony in a composition, but it must not be static. In Chinese art the painter strives for perfect rhythm in composition. His picture should have a grouping of objects in harmony so that a viewer could take out almost any part of it and still see a well balanced composition in what remains. (*See paintings* 42, 43, 44, 45, 46.)

The artist should have in mind all the important features and characteristics of his subject before he starts to work. He may then proceed to compose his picture with due regard for spacing, symmetry, and selection. Spacing may be used to emphasize the values and proportions of his subject. Unfilled portions of a picture do not necessarily represent merely empty space, for the imagination of the observer supplies the details as his thoughts are drawn from the concrete to the non-visible. The shapes of spaces may assume an importance scarcely less than the shapes of features to be portrayed, and may be made to play an integral part in composition. Proper spacing will create an inexpressible richness in calm and reposefulness. A painting should have open as well as heavily massed parts, and the open areas must be balanced in strength by the heavy elements. Proper spacing, in the words of a Chinese saying, will be "so solidly grouped that not even the wind can pass, yet so open that a horse may walk through it." (*See paintings* 48, 49, 50, 51, 53, 54, 55, 56, 57, 58.)

The concept of symmetry should not be taken to indicate that there will always be complete equilibrium in the arrangement of a painting. The balance required is not one of absolute symmetry, but involves rather an artistic license of variation. Complete regularity of form and arrangement should usually be avoided. If a painter places two trees in his landscape, one should be made taller than the other. Two rocks of the same size and shape produce a much less interesting effect than those

Opposite: Painting 47. Chrysanthemums. Six pictures illustrate the importance of spacing and the development of loose and heavy masses. These principles are used in Chinese flower arrangement as well as in painting; the artist can rearrange branches and clusters of flowers to produce just the effect he desires.

which show irregularity. In fact the principle of irregularity should prevail in the arrangement of subject matter. Subordination of some parts of a subject tends to create rhythm which is mobile and temporal. There must be full recognition of the relations of principal and subordinate parts of a subject if this sound rule of composition is to be successfully applied. (*See paintings* 47, 52.)

A painter need not always reproduce exactly what he sees in a landscape, nor the grouping of all of the objects present. He must learn to select the mountains, the expanses of water, the human figures which are of primary interest and which are most suitable to the subject of his painting. He must build his picture around the essentials. In acquiring this skill of selectivity there is no substitute for constant observation, practice sketching, studying what other artists have done to produce pleasing results. A sense of values must be developed. A distinguishing contrast of color or form can make some features outstanding in contrast to their surroundings. And it must be borne in mind that "the hand cannot execute what the mind has not experienced."

While it is hard to formulate a set of rules, the following procedure may be recommended to the artist wishing to paint a landscape. At the outset he should study the scene as a whole; he must decide, before he takes up his brushes and colors, which elements are vital and interesting, and be prepared to omit those which are not. If many objects are included, the painting may become cluttered and too "busy." Such "spottiness" involves a violation of the basic principles of composition. In composing his painting, the artist must always be concerned with balance, harmony, and proper spacing. Life and movement must be depicted with a minimum of strokes if his work is to have a dynamic quality. He should paint rapidly and confidently, and yet with restraint.

It was the desire of Chinese artists in early times to express a continuity of life, a spirit of immortality. Nature provided both the subjects and the inspiration. In our later years we must still turn to the world about us if we are to acquire the feeling for design and rhythm that characterizes the work of the old masters.

Opposite: Painting 48. Doves. These four compositions, which exhibit heavy massing, loose structure, and high and low parts, represent another lesson on grouping and spacing. Evenness of height and excess of material are undesirable.

滿布當空留之地.

此群鴿示示佈局之道或飛或立姿態不同宜在疏密相間高下參差忌星羅棋佈.

若佈滿必畫飄搖之態。

鴨首附近，決不能再作他物，否則壅塞失玲瓏意景。左圖細柳絲二空間多留空白地位，

一畫之章法，最不宜全部佈滿，必須多留空白地位。此二畫皆于空白安尋求畫意。右圖

Paintings 49 and 50. Autumn Willow; Ducks. Here again the importance of spacing is to be noted. In the example on page 62 the grace and beauty of the willow branches could not be seen if there were not empty spaces. In the painting on this page the eye is drawn immediately to the heads of the two ducks, which have clarity and brilliance because of the empty space around them.

印空白山此畫用雲霧以作空白。
圖虎若些雲霧則洞塞矣故一畫湏呂君呂寅窓
此圖应注意于雲霧盖全幅重岩叠嶂又呂叢林

Painting 51. "Visit to the Temple." Since this landscape is composed of many subjects, it was necessary to break up the heavy massing of the mountains and trees. Mist was introduced to give a feeling of space between the two groups; otherwise, the mountains would appear top-heavy.

呆枝之象，
石伏三五成群錯落呂徵不使呂
仍呂疎窓又石右二叢之樹石高
繁枝雜弊定窓的何而水洞天空

Painting 52. "A Winter Scene." The tree on the left with its trunk and many branches indicates the heavy massed area in this composition. The sky and water serve as empty space which sets off the trees. The small tree on the right indicates the lower level of the hill. This is another example of grouping, spacing, and picturing different levels in a landscape.

為學者言之蓋疏密虛實為佈局亦要之道也。

此六圖或上重下輕或在多右少要在多幅俱要疏密古人云疏可容馬密不透風一再

Paintings 53, 54, 55, 56, 57, and 58. Birds, Flowers, and Landscapes. Six compositions exemplifying compact arrangement and proper spacing. Note how the heavy structure may be above or below, at right or left in the composition.

Chapter 10

SIMPLICITY

Stroke has been discussed as an inherent part of Chinese painting in Chapter 6. We may now consider one of the essential features of a stroke, its simplicity. The Chinese consider simplicity to be the epitome of refinement. Li Cheng had this in mind when he said, "Ink is as valuable as gold." He did not use excess ink, or many strokes. He was working for simplicity. Chinese art is subjective and highly symbolical. Overemphasis of its implications would be vulgar. Furthermore, the Chinese method of painting from memory is most effective in eliminating immaterial details. So the absence of ostentation and complexity in line, color, and design has come to be the rule for a successful painting, and accounts for its sincerity and naturalness. (*See paintings* 59, 60, 65, 66.)

Paintings 59 and (*opposite*) 60. Crane; Lotus and Kingfisher. Two pictures demonstrating simplicity in composition and stroke. To obtain this quality all unrelated or non-essential strokes must first be eliminated. Only those strokes that are absolutely necessary to form each object are left in the paintings. Then, with care, a few embellishments are added in appropriate places.

此二圖供用減筆寫成簡之入微助洗老塵漢學簡之法有先畫一物試減去二三次再減

一二待減墨可減印成簡筆畫學者應練習之

The free-flowing stroke in a beautiful picture looks almost careless, but in reality is the result of long years of laborious drills and exercises. Great art is always simple, never obscure and confused. To say much with little is its highest aim. When there are many details in a painting, the beauty of strokes and the harmony of colors cannot be seen. The qualities of living beauty and spontaneity in a painting do not come as accidents, but are carefully planned. (*See paintings* 61, 62, 63.)

Keeping simplicity in mind, an artist must exercise great care in executing strokes and in his use of color. A "busy" painting with redundancy of strokes is the work of an amateur. It may not be easy for the young painter to achieve simplicity of stroke and design, but young and old alike should strive for it. The more unpretentious the motif, the better. Proper spacing and restraint in arrangement provide the framework for high expression; an empty area can be made eloquent. (*See paintings* 64, 67, 68.)

To summarize, the artist should aim for sparseness in the number of features used to convey his ideas. The fundamental value of simplicity cannot be over-emphasized.

Painting 61. Fish. A study plate showing essential strokes in the painting of a fish. The first stroke makes the upper part of the body; the second forms the belly; finally the head, tail, and fins are added. The first and second strokes are executed quickly in order to obtain a watery appearance, and close together so they blend into a single unit instead of appearing as two distinct sections. The other parts of the fish can be painted separately at a more leisurely pace.

Painting 62. "Swimming Group." The fish in this picture were painted by the simple method demonstrated above.

Painting 63. "Swimming Pair." A third example of fish painting done in the same manner. After the two fish were outlined and the colors had dried, a wide brush was used to paint the surrounding water.

Painting 64. Catfish. The shape of these fish required a slightly different technique. With a very wet brush several light strokes were blended together on the paper. Darker areas were added while the first strokes were still wet. The simplicity of the composition resembles the other examples shown on these pages.

及過切而成小扁矣頭胸背三筆而用淡墨定體嘴眼翼尾而用濃墨簡筆作小鳥法二作頭二加胸三補背待頭胸背完成已為鳥之雛形矣再加嘴眼翼尾

Painting 65. Birds. This study plate demonstrates the easiest way to paint a small bird. The first stroke makes the head, the second forms the breast, and the third shapes the back. These three parts produce the shape of an egg, which comprises the body of the bird. Then the beak, eye, wing, tail, and feet are added. Light color was used for the first group of strokes and dark color for the details.

Painting 66. Birds on a Willow Branch. Painted in the same manner as shown on the opposite page.

此用前述簡筆作兩鳥法所寫成之二鳥再補疏柳但看墨紫多而意趣自豐

此三年此畫張作於金門 [seal]

此点萬簡筆畫也若柳葉太多則與鳥身混雜不能分此隆晰矣

Painting 67. "Waiting." To keep the bird as the center of interest here, just a few willow branches and leaves were added to produce a simple background in the same tones of color.

Opposite: Painting 68. Dove. The bird is perched on a branch of quince with blossoms and leaves. The design employs contrasting bold and soft strokes and colors.

此用減筆寫鴿及蠟梅，如筆渲至意趣，尤在梅枝夾渲挺秀，應求繪像本身呈現之價值，不僅湊成花枝而已也。

73

Chapter 11

BACKGROUNDS

Background work may be effectively employed to induce perspective. During the T'ang and Sung dynasties it was customary for artists to paint in background scenes to provide spatial depth. At this time silk was being used, and there was no difficulty in executing strokes to delineate clouds, mountains, and streams. But after the invention of paper and its use by artists, it was impossible to continue the use of backgrounds, for the paper was an absorbent type not suited to line painting. So in this period abstract design was used to depict distant features. Eventually a non-absorbent paper was produced, and from that time on the artist could paint anything he desired.

For background washes, select a wide brush and apply the pigments faintly, with overlapping strokes so as to leave no lines of demarcation. This smooth and even background should be set aside to dry before the foreground features are painted in. (*See paintings* 69, 70, 71, 72, 73, 74.)

先用淡青渲染作月待乾後再寫花枝所要注意者

塗背景時不可露筆痕絹本或礬紙可作此若宣紙則不宜

先塗背景，再用水墨寫渡鶴及松樹，最後用白粉染之。染白粉須有濃淡，方不致平板。

Painting 70. Snow Pine. Here again the background was painted in light blue. After this had dried, subtle tones of ink were used to paint the pine tree and the cranes. Finally white pigment was applied sparingly on certain parts and more heavily on others to avoid a stiff appearance.

Opposite: Painting 69. Pear Blossoms. The sky was first painted in a light blue color. Lines of demarcation were avoided and carefully overlapped strokes made a smooth, even background. When the paint was completely dry, the branches and blossoms were added.

待完全乾後再作睡蓮及其他。
先用綠色（即黄青調合）塗背景。

Painting 71. Water Lilies. Green (made from yellow and blue, with a touch of black) was used for the background. When this was thoroughly dry the water lilies were painted with white and tints of red.

部分,乾後再加之色,故全幅覺調和.
淡綠淡珠混合之色,滿帋塗之,惟須留雲霧之
用墨水留出石樹木及人物.在末着色以前即用

Painting 72. "Misty Mountains." In this landscape the mountains and trees were painted first, then light green and touches of brown filled the background, except for the cloud areas. When the painting was dry, the two figures at left were added and various finishing touches were made to accent the outlines and colors.

Painting 73. "Autumn River." Two dishes of pigment were prepared for the background here: one filled with light green, the other with a mixture of brown and yellow. First the green pigment was washed into the paper with spaces left for the brown-yellow areas. Slightly overlapping strokes allowed the two colors to blend, avoiding a stiff dividing line, which would have been undesirable.

此幅背景與睡蓮不同睡蓮係淡綠一種色此則用
二色，預備二碟，一盛淡綠一盛淡碟（另墨加黃）
先用淡綠橫塗之空存一二寸次用淡碟將空存其
塗滿，唯乘店濕，快揠二色之間不能見痕迹。

78

此背景則用三色須用三碟免碟
各別調以淡綠淡紅淡殊頂備好
皮用排筆以淡殊先塗工部次
用淡紅末用淡綠由工至下橫塗之
恐成日暮斜陽之景

Painting 74. "Autumn Birches." For the background wash in this sunset scene, three colors were used—light green, light brown, and light red. The colors were laid on and blended with a wide brush. The foreground was painted later with a pointed brush, using opaque white for the trunks of the trees and for the breast and wing tips of the bird.

A FINAL COMMENT ON OBJECTIVES

The Chinese art student goes through many years of training. He submits himself to intensive instruction, to long hours of practice, to arduous drills and exercises directed toward perfection of technique. At the end of this period he must have learned not alone the methods of painting. He will have come to know that the true function of art is fundamentally to train the mind to high thinking, and the heart to worthy sentiments.